King Arthur's Sword

David Calcutt

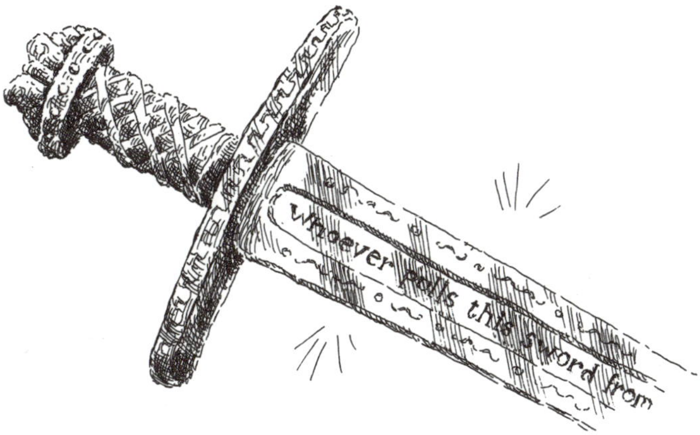

Illustrated by Anna C. Leplar

OXFORD
UNIVERSITY PRESS

OXFORD
UNIVERSITY PRESS

Great Clarendon Street, Oxford OX2 6DP

Oxford University Press is a department of the University of Oxford.
It furthers the University's objective of excellence in research, scholarship,
and education by publishing worldwide in

Oxford New York

Auckland Bangkok Buenos Aires Cape Town Chennai
Dar es Salaam Delhi Hong Kong Istanbul Karachi Kolkata
Kuala Lumpur Madrid Melbourne Mexico City Mumbai Nairobi
São Paulo Shanghai Singapore Taipei Tokyo Toronto

with an associated company in Berlin

Oxford is a registered trade mark of Oxford University Press
in the UK and in certain other countries

First published 2002

British Library Cataloguing in Publication Data

Data available

ISBN 0 19 915924 6

10 9 8 7 6 5 4 3 2 1

Also available in packs
Years 5–6 Playscripts Mixed Pack (one of each playscript) ISBN 0 19 917899 2
Years 5–6 Playscripts Guided Reading Pack King Arthur's Sword (six copies) ISBN 0 19 915930 0

Design by Sue Clarke

Cover illustration by Jane Bottomley

Printed in Hong Kong

Cast list

(in order of appearance)

Tom *a boy lost on Merlin's Hill*

Morgana *King Arthur's half-sister; the storyteller*

Merlin *a wise and powerful magician*

Uther Pendragon *the King of England*

Ector *a loyal subject of the king*

Sir Bors

Sir Ban

two knights who try to pull the sword from the stone

Kay *Ector's eldest son; he is bossy and boastful*

Arthur *Ector's adopted younger son; his real father is Uther Pendragon*

Sir Balin *a knight who tries to pull the sword from the stone*

Father *Tom's father*

Scene 1

A hilltop in England, about five hundred years ago. There is a large stone on one side of the stage. **Tom** *enters. He has just climbed the hill. He is lost and tired. He speaks aloud to himself.*

Tom I'm so tired. This hill is so steep. I must rest. There's a stone. I'll sit on that. *(He sits down on the stone)* What am I going to do? I'm lost and I don't know the way back. I wish someone was here.

***Morgana** enters. She wears a cloak and carries a wooden staff. She speaks to **Tom**.*

Morgana Why are you sitting on that stone?

***Tom** turns to **Morgana** and gives a gasp of surprise. He jumps up.*

Tom I was tired. I wanted to rest. I've just climbed this hill.

Morgana I see. What's your name?

Tom Tom.

Morgana And where do you live, Tom?

Tom In a village, a long way from here.

Morgana But now you're lost, and tired. And hungry and thirsty as well, I suppose.

Tom Yes, I am.

Morgana I'm afraid I don't have any food with me, but if you look behind the stone *(She points at the stone)* you'll see a small spring of fresh water.

Tom looks behind the stone.

Morgana Do you see it?

Tom Yes.

Morgana Drink some water. You'll find it very refreshing.

Tom drinks from the spring.

Tom It's delicious! I'm not thirsty or hungry anymore! It's like magic!

Morgana It's not *like* magic. It *is* magic. The spring's magic, the stone you were sitting on is magic. This whole hill is magic, inside and out.

Tom Are you magic too?

Morgana Yes, I am. My name is Morgana. Once I was a queen. Now I look after this hill, and the story that lies inside it. It's an ancient story, sleeping deep beneath the ground, and you have woken it.

Tom How have I woken it?

Morgana By sitting on that stone. You sat there and said 'I wish someone was here'. The stone granted your wish. It brought me – and I will bring you the story. Sit, now. Listen and watch.

__Tom__ sits as __Morgana__ tells the story.

Morgana This story comes from a long time ago, just after the Romans had left our land, and Uther Pendragon was king. He had a hard time fighting against the Saxons who came across the sea, but he ruled well with the help of a powerful magician called Merlin.

__Uther__ and __Merlin__ enter.

Uther Merlin, since I became king I've had to fight against the Saxons. They burned our towns and killed our people, but with your help I defeated them. Now I need your help again.

Merlin I'll give it, if you tell me why.

Uther Some of my own people have betrayed me. They've joined forces with the Saxons, and I'm not strong enough to defeat them. I don't care about my own life, but I do care about the life of my son.

Merlin So you're asking me to protect him, if you're killed?

Uther Yes.

Merlin Then you must give him to me now and I'll take him away. He'll be raised in secret, and no one will know who he is.

Uther Who'll raise him? You?

Merlin No – though I will watch over him. There's a man who's always been faithful to you, and who will be faithful to your son. That man is Ector.

Uther Ector, yes. He's a good friend.

Merlin He'll raise the child as his own. Only he and I will know whose son he really is. He will grow up in safety, until he's old enough to be king.

Uther But how can you be sure of that? Some of my enemies are strong and powerful. What if one of them makes himself king while my son is still a child?

Merlin No one will become king until your son does. I shall see to that.

Uther With your magic?

Merlin With my magic.

Uther Then I know that my son will be safe – and that the country will be safe too, in his hands, and yours.

__Merlin__ and __Uther__ go off in different directions.

Scene 2

***Morgana** continues her story.*

Morgana So Merlin took the child in secret to Ector, and my poor father was killed in battle.

Tom King Uther was your father?

Morgana That's right.

Tom So his child must be your brother.

Morgana My half-brother. We had different mothers. And from the moment Merlin took him away, I didn't see him again until he was king, because no one, not even I, knew where he was.

Tom He did become king, then?

Morgana Yes. He became king. Watch, now, and see how it came about.

***Merlin** enters carrying a sword. **Ector** follows him.*

Ector Uther's child will be safe with me, Merlin. My wife and I shall raise him with our own son. And no one shall know that they aren't true brothers, not even the boys themselves.

Merlin Thank you, Ector. Now that Uther is dead, there are troublesome times ahead. Many wish to become king, and they'll stop at nothing to get the crown.

Ector But how do you intend to stop them?

Merlin I won't stop them. This sword shall.

Merlin holds up the sword.

Ector That sword? You're no fighter, Merlin–

Merlin I know. I shan't be fighting with it. Take it, Ector. There are some words written on the blade. What do they say?

Ector takes the sword and reads aloud the words written on the blade.

Ector 'Whoever pulls this sword from this stone, is the right and true-born King of England.' *(To* ***Merlin****)* I don't understand.

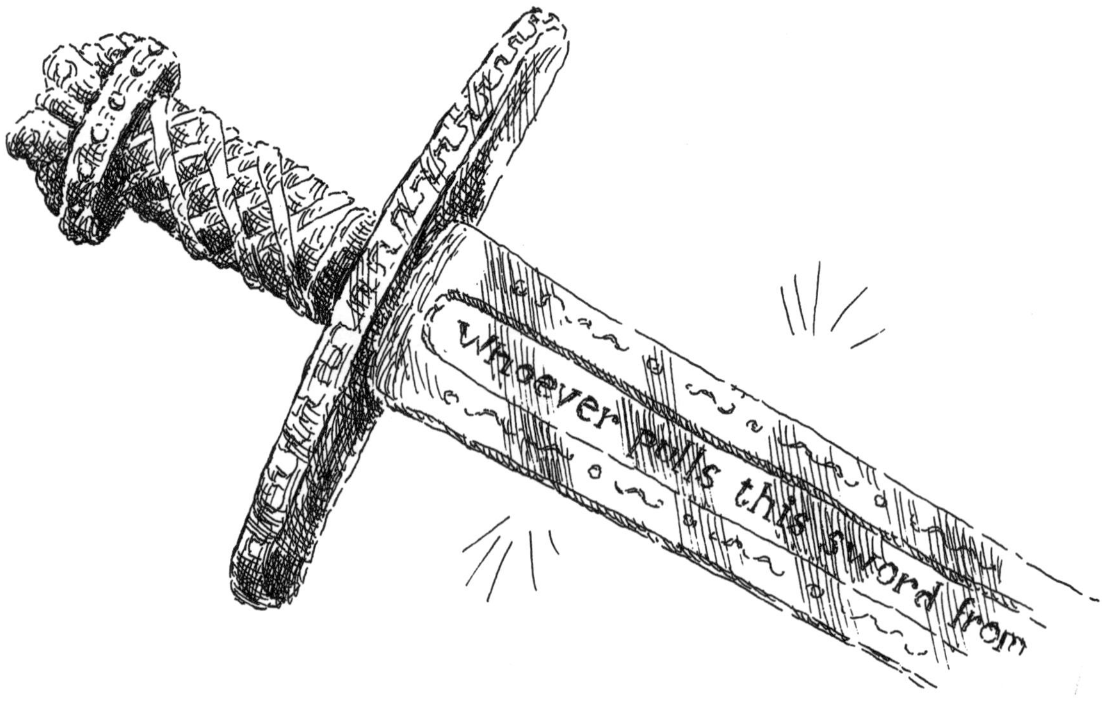

Merlin I'll show you. Give the sword back to me.

__Ector__ gives the sword back to __Merlin__. __Merlin__ pushes the sword into the stone as he speaks.

Merlin Whoever pulls *this* sword from *this* stone, is the right and true-born King of England.

__Merlin__ releases the sword and stands back. The sword stands up out of the stone.

Merlin There. It is done.

Ector So if someone pulls the sword out of the stone, he will become king?

Merlin Yes.

Ector And what's to stop anyone from pulling it out?

Merlin Try it yourself. Pull the sword out. Become king.

Ector I don't want to be king.

Merlin You won't be king, don't worry. Go on.

Ector Very well.

***Ector** takes hold of the sword. He pulls, but it won't come out of the stone.*

Merlin Having trouble?

Ector Yes ... it seems to be a little stuck ... I'll have it free in a minute, though ...

***Ector** keeps pulling, but he can't get the sword out.*

Merlin Still stuck?

Ector Yes! It's no good! I can't move it!

***Ector** lets go of the sword.*

Merlin And neither will anyone else – except the true-born king.

Ector Arthur.

Merlin Who?

Ector Arthur. That is what we call Uther's son.

Merlin Arthur. Yes. It's a good name. And when he pulls the sword from the stone, he shall be King of England.

Ector And when will that be?

Merlin It will be – when it will be. Now I must leave you. I have many things to do, and a long way to travel. But I shall return, and on that day there will be cause for great celebration.

***Merlin** and **Ector** go.*

Scene 3

***Morgana** continues the story.*

Morgana Many people tried to pull the sword out of the stone. Especially the strong and powerful ones. None of them could, but this did not stop them trying. In fact, they made a great festival out of it. Once a year, all the powerful lords of the land would gather together at the place where the stone stood. They'd have archery competitions and displays of sword-fighting and wrestling matches. And then, later in the day, the strongest and most powerful knights would try and pull the sword out of the stone.

***Sir Bors** and **Sir Ban** enter noisily.*

Sir Bors Stand back! Make way for the true-born King of England!

Sir Ban Oh, yes? And who's that?

Sir Bors Me! Or I will be, just as soon as I've pulled out this sword.

Sir Ban You think you can pull it out?

Sir Bors Of course I can! I'm the strongest knight here! Watch!

Sir Bors tries to pull out the sword. He tries and tries but he can't move it.

Sir Bors I don't understand it. I was sure I'd be able to pull it out.

Sir Ban And I was sure you wouldn't.

Sir Bors Why?

Sir Ban Because you're not the true-born King of England. I am. Step aside, please.

Sir Bors moves to one side. *Sir Ban* takes hold of the sword.

Sir Ban Now watch, and see how it's done.

Sir Ban tries to pull out the sword, but it remains stuck.

Sir Bors I see. That's how it's done, is it?

Sir Ban Bother! It looks like neither of us is the true-born king.

Sir Bors How disappointing! Let's go back to my castle and cheer ourselves up with a feast.

Sir Ban Good idea! Then we'll go to mine and have another.

***Sir Bors** and **Sir Ban** go. **Morgana** continues the story.*

Morgana And when they'd all tried and failed, they'd go home and wait until next year.

Tom What about Arthur?

Morgana He didn't know anything about it. Ector never went to these festivities. He wanted to make sure no one knew about Arthur until the time was right.

***Kay** enters, carrying a bow and a quiver.*

Morgana Years passed and Arthur grew up thinking that Ector was his father, and that Ector's son, Kay, was his brother. *(She points to **Kay**)* Kay was older than Arthur – and, I'm afraid to say, very bossy.

***Kay** turns and calls off stage.*

Kay Come on, Arthur! Hurry up, will you? I want to practise my archery.

***Arthur** enters.*

Arthur Here I am, Kay.

Kay It's about time. Why do you have to be so slow? I always have to wait for you.

Arthur Sorry.

Kay One of these days I won't wait. I'll leave you behind and you'll get lost, and eaten by wolves or killed by outlaws. That will serve you right. Here. Hold this.

*He gives **Arthur** the quiver.*

Kay I'm going to practise my archery here, in this clearing. Pass me an arrow when I tell you to. All right?

Arthur Yes.

Kay Go on, then.

Arthur What?

Kay Pass me an arrow!

Arthur Now?

Kay Yes, now! You really are slow, aren't you?

Arthur Sorry. Here.

***Arthur** passes **Kay** an arrow – point first.*

Kay Not like that, idiot! The sharp point's facing towards me. Turn it round, so the point's facing away from me.

Arthur Oh ... *(**Arthur** turns the arrow round and offers it to **Kay**)* Like this?

Kay Yes. *(He takes the arrow)* Now, you see that tree over there?

Arthur Which tree?

Kay *(Pointing)* That one. The big oak tree, at the furthest edge of the clearing.

Arthur Oh, yes.

Kay I'm going to put this arrow right in the middle of it. Keep your eyes on me. You're going to see a real archer at work. First, I fit the arrow to the string *(He fits the arrow in the string)* ... then I raise the bow *(He raises the bow)* ... pull back the string *(He pulls back the string)* ... take aim *(He takes aim)* ... and fire! *(He fires)*

Arthur You missed.

Kay What?

Arthur Look.

__Kay__ looks.

Arthur You missed the tree.

Kay I can see that. It was your fault.

Arthur My fault? Why?

Kay You moved just when I fired.

Arthur No, I didn't–

Kay I say you did! And I'm older than you, and bigger, so I must be right. You put me off, and now I've lost the arrow. Go and find it now!

Arthur But–

Kay Don't argue with me! Give me my arrows back and go and find the one you lost! And don't come back until you have!

***Arthur** gives the quiver back to **Kay** and walks off stage to look for the arrow. **Kay** speaks aloud to himself.*

Kay What an idiot! Fancy having a fool like that for a brother! I'll teach him a lesson. I'll go home now and leave him here. He can find his own way back. And if he gets lost … well, that's his own fault.

__Kay__ goes off in a different direction. __Arthur__ enters calling.

Arthur Kay! Kay! Where are you? Don't hide. I'm scared. Kay! There might be wolves. Or bears. Or bandits. Or–

__Merlin__ enters. __Arthur__ sees him and gasps in surprise.

Arthur Oh! Who are you?

Merlin My name is Merlin. Who are *you*?

Arthur My name's Arthur.

Merlin Arthur, is it? Tell me, Arthur. Do you have a father?

Arthur Yes, of course I do.

Merlin And what's his name?

Arthur His name is Ector.

Merlin Ector! And you're his son, Arthur. Arthur, son of Ector. It *is* you. I thought it was, but I couldn't be sure. You've grown. Of course, you have. The last time I saw you, you were a babe in arms. And now look at you. Almost a man. Tell me, Arthur. How is Ector? Is he well?

Arthur Very well, thank you, sir ... you know my father, then?

Merlin Oh, yes! I know him very well. Ector and I are old friends. It's time we met again. Come along.

Arthur Where?

Merlin Home, of course. Your home.

Arthur Do you know where it is?

Merlin Of course I do. You might get lost in the forest, but I don't. I know every path, every track. And if we hurry, we can be there before that young rascal, Kay. That'll wipe the grin off his face. Come on. Come along. Hurry!

***Merlin** and **Arthur** go.*

Scene 4

***Morgana** continues the story.*

Morgana It was almost Christmas, the time when all the knights gathered near the place where the stone stood to see if anyone could draw the sword. And now that Merlin had returned, Ector knew that it was time for Arthur to take his place as the King of England. So he told Kay and Arthur that this year they were going to the festivities. Kay was especially excited, and couldn't stop talking about it.

***Kay** and **Arthur** enter.*

Kay We're almost there. Now that Father's made me a knight, I can take part in the competitions, and I'm going to take part in all of them. And win them as well. The archery competition, I'll win that easily. And the wrestling. I'm really good at wrestling.

***Kay** grabs hold of **Arthur** and twists his arm behind his back.*

Kay See?

Arthur Let go!

Kay You can't get free, can you?

Arthur No!

Kay I could throw you now. Just flip you right over, if I wanted to. But I don't want to.

Arthur Kay!

Kay What?

Arthur You're hurting! Let me go!

Kay All right.

Kay lets Arthur go.

Kay I shouldn't really be fighting with you, anyway. You're not a knight. Knights only fight with other knights.

Arthur Why hasn't Father made me a knight?

Kay Because you're too young. And too weak, as well. And too stupid. You could never win any competition, even if they let you take part. Not like me. I'll win the archery competition. And the wrestling competition.

Arthur Is there a boasting competition as well?

Kay What did you say? A boating competition? Of course there isn't! We're not anywhere near a river or a lake, you idiot! You've made me forget what I was saying, now.

Arthur You were talking about all the competitions you're going to win.

Kay Oh, yes! That's right. Archery, wrestling and sword-fighting. I'm sure to win that. I've really been practising my sword-play. Look, I'll show you.

Kay reaches down to take his sword from his belt, but then stops.

Kay Where is it? My sword? What's happened to it?

Arthur I don't know–

Kay It's gone – someone's stolen it–

Arthur How can someone have stolen it? We haven't seen anyone on the journey.

Kay Where is it, then? Where's my sword?

Arthur Perhaps you left it at home.

Kay Left it at home? Of course I didn't. Do you really think I'd do something as stupid as that? I'm not an idiot like you, you know. I definitely remember putting it on. It was the last thing I did before we left. I put the sword in the belt, and then I put the belt around my waist–

Arthur And then Father told you to put an extra coat on because it was cold.

Kay That's right, so I took the belt off again and put an extra coat on–

He stops.

Arthur And left the belt and the sword behind.

Kay Idiot!

Arthur What?

Kay You! You fool! You idiot! It was your fault.

Arthur How?

Kay You should have reminded me to put it back on again.

Arthur How did I know you hadn't put it back on again?

Kay You should have known! It's your fault I left it behind, so *you'll* have to go back and get it!

Arthur Go all the way back home?

Kay Yes.

Arthur It's miles away.

Kay It shouldn't take you long if you run.

Arthur I can't run all the way there and back.

Kay Yes, you can – and you will. I must have my sword, and you have to fetch it. So you'd better set off now. The sooner you start, the sooner you'll be back.

***Kay** starts to walk off. **Arthur** calls after him.*

Arthur Kay–!

*Kay goes. **Arthur** talks aloud to himself.*

Arthur It isn't fair! It was Kay's fault he left his sword at home, not mine. Just because he's bigger and stronger than me, he thinks he can order me about. And that just isn't fair, or right. But there's nothing I can do about it. He must have his sword, so I suppose I have to go and fetch it.

***Arthur** goes.*

Scene 5

***Morgana** continues the story.*

Morgana So Arthur set off back home and Kay went on to the festivities.

Tom Did he win any of the competitions?

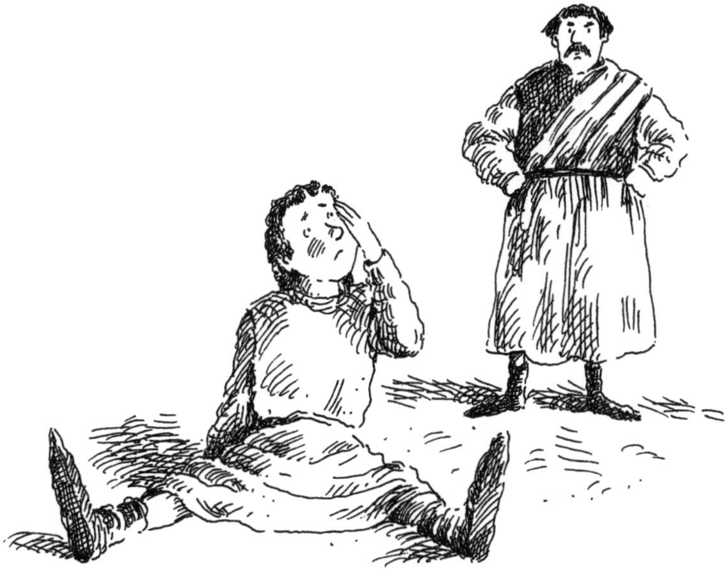

Morgana No. And at the end of the day, when some of the knights gathered to try and pull the sword from the stone, Arthur still hadn't returned.

***Kay** enters, with **Ector** and **Sir Balin**.*

Ector It's your turn to try now, Sir Balin – if you wish to.

Sir Balin Of course I wish to. I've kept the secret hidden for long enough.

Ector What secret?

Sir Balin That I'm the true-born King of England. I dreamed it when I was a boy, and I've known since then.

Ector I see. Very well, now's your chance to prove it to us.

Sir Balin I intend to. And I'm so certain I'll pull that sword out that I'll just use one hand.

***Sir Balin** takes hold of the sword with one hand and tries to pull it out, but it doesn't move.*

Sir Balin Perhaps I'll use two hands.

__Sir Balin__ takes hold of the sword with both hands and tries hard to pull it out, but it still doesn't move.

Sir Balin It's no good. I just can't move it. It looks like my brother was right after all.

Ector Your brother?

Sir Balin My twin brother. We both had the same dream when we were young, and we used to argue about whose dream was true and whose wasn't. It looks like it was his after all.

Ector Is your brother here?

Sir Balin Yes, he's waiting in the field. I'll just go and fetch him.

__Sir Balin__ goes. __Ector__ turns to __Kay__.

Ector I'm surprised Arthur isn't here. Do you know where he is, Kay?

Kay Didn't I tell you?

Ector No. I haven't seen you all day.

Kay When we arrived here this morning I found I'd forgotten my sword, so Arthur went back to fetch it.

Ector You made him go all the way back home?

Kay I didn't make him. In fact, I tried to stop him, but he insisted on going.

Ector It's a long way. I hope he gets back soon.

Kay So do I. I want my sword.

***Sir Balin** enters wearing a false beard. He pretends to be his twin brother, Sir Balan.*

Sir Balin Here I am, ready to pull the sword from the stone.

Ector You're Balin's twin brother?

Sir Balin That's right.

Ector And what's your name?

Sir Balin Balan.

Ector That's the same name as your brother.

Sir Balin No, it isn't. His name's Balin, and my name's Balan. Balin. Balan. They're completely different names.

Ector I see. You look just like him, you know. Apart from the beard.

Sir Balin We *are* twins.

Ector *(Playing along)* Of course. All right, then. Try and pull the sword out of the stone.

Sir Balin I won't even have to try.

***Sir Balin** takes hold of the sword and tries to pull it out. It won't move. He keeps on trying.*

Sir Balin It's moving. I can feel it. Any minute now it will come out. Just one more pull.

Ector I've had an idea. Why don't you go and ask your brother to help you?

Sir Balin *(Letting go of the sword)* My brother?

Ector Yes. As you're twins, and you both had the same dream, perhaps you're meant to be kings together.

Sir Balin I don't think so.

Ector Go on, bring him here. I'm sure the two of you will be able to pull it out.

Sir Balin I can't bring him here.

Ector Why not?

Sir Balin Er … he won't come. He's sulking because he didn't pull the sword out.

Ector I'll go and find him. I'm sure if I speak to him he'll come.

Sir Balin No! You can't. You won't be able to find him.

Ector Why not?

Sir Balin Because … because …

Ector Because you haven't got a brother, have you? You aren't twins. There's just you.

Sir Balin How dare you! Of course there are two of us. I have a beard–

Ector Come on, Balin. We both know that beard's not real.

Ector pulls Sir Balin's beard off and gives it to him.

Sir Balin All right, I admit it. I just wanted to have another go. I was sure I'd be able to pull it out a second time.

Ector But you couldn't, and you wouldn't be able to, no matter how many times you tried. Only the true-born king will be able to pull the sword out of the stone, and that's not you.

Sir Balin You're right. It's not me. But who is it? That's what I want to know. And when are we going to find him? Our land's been without a king for too long.

Ector It has, and I hope we'll find one soon. But not today, it seems. Come along, let's go to our tents. It's late, and I want my supper.

Kay Wait a minute, Father. What about me?

Ector What do you mean?

Kay Perhaps I'm the true-born king.

Ector You?

Kay I might be.

Ector Don't be ridiculous.

Kay You won't know if you don't let me try. And I'm a knight, now, so you have to let me.

Sir Balin Your boy's right. If he's a knight, he has to have his turn.

Ector Oh, very well, Kay. Take hold of the sword and try and pull it out.

Kay tries but he can't pull the sword out.

Ector Are you happy now?

Kay No. Let me have one more go.

Ector You've had your go. One turn each, those are the rules. *(Sternly to **Sir Balin**)* Aren't they, Balin, or Balan, or whatever your name is?

Sir Balin Oh, yes, quite right. Never mind, lad, better men than you have tried to pull out the sword and failed. Much, much better men.

***Kay**, **Ector** and **Sir Balin** go.*

Scene 6

***Morgana** continues the story.*

Morgana Some time later, when the knights had all returned to their tents, and the fires were burning and supper was cooking, Arthur arrived – without Kay's sword.

Tom Why didn't he have it?

Morgana When he got back home he found the whole house locked up. All the servants had gone on holiday, and he couldn't get in.

Arthur *enters and speaks aloud to himself.*

Arthur I don't know what I'm going to do. Kay will be really angry if I don't bring him a sword. But where can I find one? It's almost night and–

He stops and sees the sword in the stone.

Arthur How strange. A sword sticking up out of a stone. I wonder who left it there? *(He approaches the sword)* It can't have been here long. It looks brand new. I wonder if I could just borrow it? Kay can use it in the competition tomorrow, and then I can put it back again. No one will ever know. Yes. That's what I'll do. I'll take this one.

Arthur pulls the sword easily out of the stone. He holds it up.

Arthur That's odd. It looks heavy, but it feels so light. And I somehow feel right holding it. Almost as if–

Kay enters and interrupts Arthur.

Kay Arthur! What are you doing here? *(He sees the sword)* And what are you doing with that sword?

Arthur It's yours.

Kay Mine? Let me see. *(He takes the sword)* This isn't my sword. Where did you get it? Did you pull it out of the stone?

Arthur Yes.

Kay You shouldn't really have done that, Arthur. Only knights are allowed to take this sword, and you're not a knight, are you?

Arthur No.

Kay And if anybody finds out you took it, you'll be in trouble. Big trouble.

Arthur I didn't mean to do anything wrong. I couldn't get your sword, so I borrowed this one. I did it for you–

Kay I know you did, Arthur. And I'm very grateful. And I'll tell you what I'll do for you in return. I'll tell people that I took the sword. I'm a knight, so it won't matter. That way you won't get in trouble.

Arthur You'll do that for me? Thank you, Kay.

Kay Think nothing of it. That's what big brothers are for.

***Ector** enters and speaks to **Kay**.*

Ector Kay, why have you come back here? Supper's cooked. *(He sees **Arthur**)* Arthur. You're back at last. I was beginning to get worried about you–

Kay Father! Look! *(He holds up the sword)* I did it! I pulled the sword from the stone!

Ector What?

Kay I came back for another go–

Ector You know that's not allowed–

Kay Yes, but I did feel the sword move the first time, so I wanted to try again.

Ector And the second time you managed to pull it out.

Kay I did. And here it is.

Ector So I see. Are you sure it was you who pulled it out?

Kay Yes. Ask Arthur. He was here.

Ector *(To **Arthur**)* Is it true, Arthur? Did Kay pull the sword out of the stone?

Arthur Yes.

Ector Let's make certain, then. Give me the sword for a moment, Kay.

***Kay** gives **Ector** the sword, and **Ector** pushes it back into the stone.*

Kay Father! What are you doing?

Ector If you pulled it out once, you can pull it out again. And this time I want to see you do it myself. Go on.

Kay All right. I will.

Kay takes hold of the sword and tries to pull it out. He can't.

Ector What's the matter, Kay?

Kay It's a bit stuck. I'll have it free in a minute, though.

Kay tries again and again, each time with greater effort, but he can't pull the sword free.

Ector It's no good, is it, Kay? You can't pull the sword out. And you didn't pull it out before, did you?

Kay gives up trying to pull the sword out. He turns to Ector.

Kay No. I didn't. I lied, and I'm sorry.

Ector Then who did pull the sword out of the stone?

Arthur It was me, Father.

Ector You?

Arthur Yes, but I didn't know I was doing anything wrong–

Ector Show me. Pull the sword out again.

Arthur I don't know if I'll be able to. If Kay can't–

Ector Try.

Arthur *goes up to the sword and takes hold of it.*

Ector Go on.

Arthur *pulls the sword out of the stone easily.*

Arthur I did it!

Ector Now put it back.

Arthur *puts the sword back.*

Ector Kay. Now you try again.

Kay *tries again, but he can't pull the sword out.*

Kay It's no good. It just won't move.

Ector Now I'll try.

***Ector** takes hold of the sword and pulls as hard as he can. He gasps for breath as he speaks.*

Ector You see … no matter how hard I try … even if I use all my strength … I can't pull the sword free …

He gives up and lets go.

Ector And neither can anyone else, Arthur, except you.

Arthur Me? But why? Why only me?

Ector Take the sword out again.

***Arthur** pulls the sword out.*

Ector Now look at the words written on the blade.

***Arthur** looks at the blade. As he does so, **Merlin** enters, speaking.*

Merlin Whoever pulls this sword from this stone, is the right and true-born King of England.

They all turn to ***Merlin****.*

Merlin That means you, Arthur.

Arthur Me? King of England?

Merlin Yes.

Arthur But how? I can't be! I'm not sure I want to be king!

Merlin It doesn't matter what you want. It's what you are. What you were born to be.

Ector It's true, Arthur. You are my king, and I am your loyal subject.

*Ector kneels before **Arthur**. He looks up and speaks to **Kay**.*

Ector And so is Kay.

Kay What? Oh, yes–

Kay kneels.

Arthur Please don't kneel. There's no need. Stand up. I don't want you to be my subjects. I don't want to be king. I just want everything to be like it was before.

Merlin I'm afraid it can't be, Arthur. Nothing will ever be the same again. You're no longer a boy, but a man. And not just any man, but a king, and this land needs you.

Arthur But I don't know how to be king. I don't know what to do.

Merlin Don't worry about that. That's why I'm here.

Ector and Kay stand.

Ector And we will help you as well. Won't we, Kay?

Kay Yes, of course. And, Arthur – please forgive me for all the times I was horrible to you–

Arthur Of course I forgive you, Kay. No matter what happens, you'll always be my brother.

Merlin Excellent! That's the first good thing you've done as king. You've forgiven one of your subjects! It's a good start, a most promising start. Come along, now, Arthur. It's time to present you to all the lords and knights gathered here, and to let them know they have a new king at last. And one that is most promising. Most promising, indeed!

Merlin, Arthur, Ector and Kay go.

Morgana continues the story.

Morgana And that is the story of how Arthur became King of England. The story that's buried inside this hill.

Tom But that isn't the end, is it? I mean, it can't be.

Morgana Oh, no. It's not the end. It's just the beginning. There are many, many more stories. But, for now, this one is ended. And it's time for you to go.

Tom Go where?

Morgana Back to your home, of course. Just as I must go back to mine.

Tom But I don't know how to get back home.

Morgana Your father does, though.

Tom My father?

Morgana Yes. He's come looking for you.

***Tom** stands up and looks round. As he does,*
***Morgana** goes.*

Tom Father? Where? Where is he? I can't see him! Father!

***Tom** turns back to speak to **Morgana**.*

Tom You said – oh!

*He sees that **Morgana** has gone. Tom's **Father** enters.*

Father Tom.

***Tom** turns to his **Father**.*

Tom Father.

Father There you are! Your mother and I have been so worried. We were looking for you everywhere.

Tom I'm sorry, Father. I got lost.

Father I don't know what you thought you'd find up here, on Merlin's Hill.

Tom Merlin's Hill?

Father Yes, this hill is called Merlin's Hill. And that stone there is called Arthur's Seat.

Tom Merlin's Hill? Arthur's Seat?

Father Some people say it's haunted up here. It's not a good place to be alone.

Tom But I haven't been alone.

Father Haven't you?

Tom There was a woman – her name was Morgana – and she told me a story about Arthur and Merlin–

Father And where's this woman now?

Tom She *was* here – but she disappeared, just before you came–

Father I see. Tom, I think you must have fallen asleep and dreamed this story.

Tom It seemed so real. I don't think it was a dream. One day I'll come back here, and sit on the stone again, and perhaps Morgana will appear and tell me another story about King Arthur.

Father Perhaps she will, another day. But it's getting late now, and it's time we went home. Come on, let's go.

Tom *and his* ***Father*** *go.*

The End